#2 TRAVEL WITH ME & SEE
LONDON
Petite

Hello London!
Our **Travel with Me & See Petite** series is for the tiniest of explorers! Tour the city of **London** with B and two of her dove friends as they try to help the Royal Family find their missing sceptre.
Racing around to the ticking of Big Ben's clock, will they find the missing sceptre?

Tick, tock.
Tick, tock!

EXPLORE MORE

Nancy Delevoye & Carly Wadsworth
TRAVELWITHMEANDSEE.COM

Hello, London!

Big Ben is ringing and we cannot resist,
seeing your city next on our list.

It has always been a little dream to visit the kingdom of the legendary **Queen**.

Our friend Rose, Little Dove and I planned a picnic at **Hyde Park**. But raindrops came tumbling and lightning went spark!

While taking shelter, a **Shepherd's Pie** caught our eye.
What a surprise - it is savory, not sweet!
No sugar, no berries, just mashed potatoes and meat.

Mid-bite, Rose notices a newspaper clipping.
The headline reads, "The **Royal Sceptre** Has Gone Missing!"

She whispers, "The **sceptre** is a wand with a dove up top, a symbol of peace that must not be lost."

Can you help us find the missing **sceptre**?
Exploring the city to the beat of **Big Ben's** clock,
we will search for the wand...
...tick-tock. Tick-tock!

Our first stop is the **Royals'** home, **Buckingham Palace**.
We peek through the gates as we look for clues.
But there is nothing but the tapping
from the guardsmen's shoes.

 Right now it's the **Changing of the Guard**.
To get their attention would surely be hard.

Like toy soldiers in red and gold,
they march in silence, steady and controlled.

We continue our search in the London Underground, but still the sceptre is nowhere to be found!

Off to **Wembley** where cheers fill the air.
We search the shop - no **sceptre** there!
Just footballs and flags and a scarf or two,
so onto the field we go to search for a clue.

"Watch out B!" Little Dove cries. A **football** is soaring right at my side. "Don't worry" I shout, kicking it high - the fans cheer "Goal!" as it flies through the sky.

Big Ben goes BONG! Its hands point along, reminding us tick-tock, tick-tock...

the search must go on.

We stop to think,
our feet are quite sore.

We've searched the **palace**,
the **tube**, and more.

We checked the **stadium** - still no clue.
Where in **London** should we search through?

"Perhaps the **Royal Mews**," Rose says with pride,
"The **Queen** loved her Corgis, but her horses she'd ride!"

At the Royal Mews, we meet a **Cleveland Bay**, a handsome horse of **England**, who says hello with the sound of NEEEEEEIGH.

HEY! What's that he spies glowing in the hay?
Why, it's the missing **Royal Sceptre**! We found it!

Hip, hip hooray!

Covered in diamonds, rubies so bright,
the wand is a treasure, a magical sight!
We'd love to keep it and twirl it all day,
but back with the **Crown Jewels** it must stay.

Its home is the **Tower of London**, by the **River Thames** dock.
We hurry to return it, tickety-tock!

Wait! Do you see what we spy on the **Tower Bridge**?
Why, it is the **Royals'** special carriage.

The carriage is only for **Royals** to ride,
so the **Royal** family must be inside.

The carriage rolls up to **Shakespeare's** play.
We can give them the wand back right here today.

The **Royals** sit in the front row,
patiently waiting for the start of the show.

We bow on stage,
the audience cheers,
the **Royals** smile
and wipe away tears.

"Thank you," they say, "for kindness so true.
Tomorrow at the **palace**, we'll share tea with you!"

Big Ben chimes loudly, the hour is four,
and just then, someone opens a door.

The **Royals** present us with a gemstone so bright,
a thank-you for honesty, for doing what's right.
Tick-tock. Tick-tock.
Our hearts skip a beat...
new adventures are calling from a faraway street!

Little Explorers, good job finding the missing sceptre! Can you match the below images to their names?

1. **Changing of the Guard** = Marching soldiers ceremoniously taking their places on duty.
2. **Crown Jewels** = Royal objects & treasures that are safely kept in the Tower of London.
3. **Football** = Only Americans call this sport soccer!
4. **Sceptre** = A staff or wand held by the ruling King or Queen.
5. **Shepherd's Pie** = A non-sweet pie that is made with meat and topped with mashed potatoes.

London Places

Big Ben: The nickname for the bell that chimes in Elizabeth's (clock) Tower.

Buckingham Palace: Home of the Royals in London.

Hyde Park: A large park that kings used to hunt in!

London: The capital city of England.

London Underground: The "tube", London's metro.

Royal Mews: Where the Royal horses live.

River Thames: The longest river in England.

Shakespeare's Globe: Theatre of Shakespeare's plays.

Tower Bridge: Famous drawbridge across River Thames.

Tower of London: For 600 years it was a zoo! Today it is a museum and safeguards the Crown Jewel Collection.

Wembley Stadium: So huge it could fit thousands of buses!!

and Famous Faces.

The Queen: At 96 years young Queen Elizabeth II was the longest reigning monarch in British history, a total of 70 years and 214 days.

Cleveland Bay: A breed of horse from England.

The Royals: Those who are family members of the British Monarchy.

Famous Portraits Page: From top left; Queen Victoria, a young Queen Elizabeth II, Queen Elizabeth II with Sir James Paul McCartney.

NEXT STOP...
TRAVEL WITH ME & SEE
NEW YORK

Petite

EXPLORE MORE

Text Copyright © 2025 by Nancy Delevoye. Illustrations Copyright © 2025 by Carly Wadsworth. All rights reserved. No part of this book may be reproduced, transmitted or stored in an information retrieval system in any form or by any means, graphic, electronic or mechanical, including photocopying, taping and recording, without prior written permission from the publishers. First edition printed 2025. ISBN 978-0-9600423-5-7 (paperback)
This book was typeset in Comic Sans MS, Comic Sans MS - Bold and Futura. The illustrations were done primarily with watercolor pencil, markers and ink. Very few of the illustrations were enhanced using mixed-media/graphic illustration.
Self-published by Nancy Delevoye and Carly Wadsworth. Perpignan, France & Northville, MI, USA.

Be Curious, Be an Explorer, Be a Child of the World, Be You! **TRAVELWITHMEANDSEE.COM**

www.ingramcontent.com/pod-product-compliance
Lightning Source LLC
Chambersburg PA
CBHW042144290426
44110CB00002B/107